Hello, House

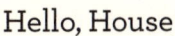

Books by Phyllis Hoge Thompson

Artichoke and Other Poems
The Creation Frame
The Serpent of the White Rose
What the Land Gave
The Ghosts of Who We Were
A Field of Poetry
Letters from Jian Hui and Other Poems
The Painted Clock: Memoir of a New Mexico Ghost Town Bride

Hello, House

POEMS BY PHYLLIS HOGE
Illustrations by Maxine Hong Kingston

Fithian Press, 2012
MCKINLEYVILLE, CALIFORNIA

Copyright © 2012 by Phyllis Hoge
Illustrations copyright © 2012 by Maxine Hong Kingston
All rights reserved
Printed in the United States of America
Library of Congress Cataloging-in-Publication Data

Hoge, Phyllis.
Hello, house : poems / by Phyllis Hoge;
illustrations by Maxine Hong Kingston.
p. cm.
ISBN 978-1-56474-524-8 (pbk. : alk. paper)
I. Kingston, Maxine Hong, ill. II. Title.
PS3608.O48267H45 2012
811'.6—dc23
     2011045742

Published by Fithian Press
A division of Daniel & Daniel, Publishers Inc.
Post Office Box 2790
McKinleyville, CA 95519
www.danielpublishing.com

Distributed by SCB Distributors (800) 729-6423
www.scbdistributors.com

Designed by Kristina Kachele Design, llc
Set in Chaparral Pro with H&FJ Archer display

DEDICATED

in loving remembrance
to my sister

Dorothy Langley Hoge Kenzie

and with gratitude for the ascendant music of her life
PH

to my Home-Loving Sisters

Carmen Hong Wong and Corinne Hong Nicolas
MHK

Hello, House

"Hello, House," my double, my self apart,
   Visible structure, body, diagram
Of my interior being, life and heart
   Disclosing, tangible sign of who I am.

A hundred "homes," a long discouraging quest,
   And a patient agent. The sudden end of mission:
"Now there's a house," I said, pleased and impressed
   By its size and age in intimate recognition.

This was my home, already familiar, plain,
   Sturdy and small. Like me. Needing fresh paint.
Comfortable. Airy. Easy to maintain.
   A simple structure. Nothing cute or quaint.

Cracks in the plaster. Springy wooden floors.
   Linoleum in the kitchen. Glassed-in shelves.
Sunshine in the bedroom. A study closed off by doors.
   Each room a metaphor for my several selves.

Fireplace—a source of passion, warmth and ease.
   For collected paintings, plenty of bare wall space.
A garden xeriscaped. A hive for bees.
   It is myself I see. I fit the place.

Here is my home. Though one day I must leave,
　I think that someone, drawn like me, will find
And welcome its happy spirit. I believe
　My house will open to a kindred mind.

And I can imagine as the years move on
A person who knows me well though I am gone.

Table Of Contents

Hello, House   7
My Front Door   13
Making The Bed   14
The Boston Cooking School Cookbook   15
Favorites   16
Artichoke   17
A Russet Potato   18
Rice   19
Dishes   20
A Daylight Discovery   22
Polishing Sugar Spoons   23
Tea and Coffee   24
Guests   25
Old Courtesies   26
Laundry   28
Stains   29
Tangible Sunshine   30
Changing Times   31
Sheets   32
Ironing Curtains   33
Cleaning the Bathroom   34
Clutter   35
Wooden Floors   36
Sweeping   38

Domestic Violence   39

Dust   40

Indoor Plants   41

An Improbable Forest   42

Holding On   44

Fireplace   45

Their Quietness   46

I Suspect My Subconscious Is On To Something   47

Dealing With the Trash   48

Recycling   49

Stitchery   50

Knitting   51

Bookworms   52

Brackets and Rods   53

Putting Up Art   54

The In-House Pet   55

The Cat and the Computer   56

Divided Joy   57

Getting the Mail   58

Noises   59

Bird Feeding   62

Cutting the Blue Gramma Grass   63

Painting the House   64

Fixers   66

Ants   67

Moths   68

Beginner's Kit: Bees   69

Packing for Travel   71

Shopping   72

Taxes   74

My Back Door   76

ACKNOWLEDGEMENTS   79

Hello, House

My Front Door

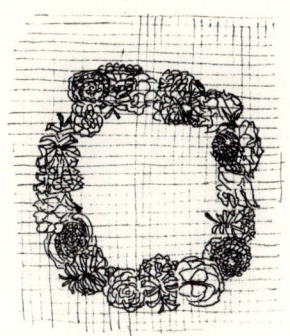

No button to push for a doorbell or for chimes.
    No knocker. A pinecone wreath behind a screen.
No means to arouse a tenant. But sometimes
    Someone will rattle the cowbell hung between
The door frame and front window. What a clang!
    A sound to command attention and evoke,
Out of a clear blue sky, the cow that rang
    That bell, loitering homeward, farmer folk
Easing her over a meadow toward the stall.
    Or someone may rap with a fist on the heavy oak frame
To force the issue.
    All anyone needs is to call.
    Odds are I'll answer. I tend to respond to my name.
If nobody seems to be here, at the backyard gate
    I might be found hanging up wash. Thing is, I might
Be hiding inside by choice, either early or late,
    Since the door allows me the option to keep out of sight.
I depend on the brass doorknob and the square brass lock
    Which open or close my house. Above is a sign
That proclaims "This house believes," bald as a rock.
    I don't know what it means. I bought it. I like it. It's mine.

Making The Bed

Bedmaking involves little more
Than pulling the covers straight up,
Tossing the pillow on top,
Adjusting the spread
From footboard to head
And putting away what you wore
The night before.

As daily as doing the dishes,
Making the bed comes before.
Change the mood of the place,
The whole indoor space
When you start out your day with this chore.
And a bed can respond to your wishes
With a couple of swishes.

The Boston Cooking School Cookbook

After all those years when I put out meals
Three times a day for four or five,
The job of cooking seldom appeals
Except as a means of staying alive.

But the *Boston Cooking School Cookbook*—
I love it. Nineteen Twenty Four
By Fannie M. Farmer, a sensible cook
Who loved the language. She had more

Fine style than many "writers." *A bit
Of bay leaf . . . and a blade of mace . . .
Force egg yolks through a strainer.* It
Burgeons with heart stopping facts—*Good geese*

Abound in pinfeathers. Dated advice:
*Use rose tube. . . . Beef should not be eaten
As soon as killed.* Instructions on spice
Go well beyond sugar or honey to sweeten,

Lemon to sour, or salt to savor.
She covers mint, marjoram, curry and sage.
All her lessons on food are dressed with the flavor
Of elegant words that garnish each page.

Favorites

I *do* still cook. I frequently ask a guest
Or two or more for dinner. Friends will get
Home-tested entrees. Brown-sugared salmon is best.
I bake it with butter and lemon. Or rich chicken tet

With mushrooms. Or layers of ham, potatoes, and cheese
In a good casserole. As accessories—basmati rice,
Asparagus, broccoli, string beans, salad or peas—
And everything fresh or one day old, if the price

Seems OK. The pleasure I take in dining with friends
I feel thankful for. And that makes me think of the great
Traditional turkey with trimmings, a bird that transcends
All other festival dinners we put on our plate,

As they did at the very first Thanksgiving feast.
                                            No doubt
I've omitted familiar favorites. But when I go out,

I tend to choose what I never have learned to cook—
Chinese, Italian, Vietnamese, and Thai,
And especially French, since at home I don't use a book
For something exotic, preferring a native standby.

We have to eat. Plain food is better than none.
But I have favorites. Artichokes are one.

Artichoke

> "When the artichoke blooms"
> Hesiod, *Works and Days,* 582

Praise love
and praise the taste of love
and raise
the thorny-pointed artichoke
coned on a prickly needled core
and tough as the gut of love.
Pour the sea-dark wine unmixed.
Pull off
the leaves
of the jagged leather
          artichoke
from around a stiffly thickened stem.
O praise the taste
of love between the teeth.
Go garlanded with parsley,
go celery-crowned to feast.
Then eat the coarse, delicious
heart of the horn,
the artichoke.

A Russet Potato

For Meredith and Tom Hughes
Curators of the Potato Museum

A russet potato is shaped like a stone.
   It's both dirty and rough, so it needs a good scrub
   Before it gets baked and turned into grub.
When some of the dirt in which it was grown
Still clings to the skin, a tap-water splatter
   Will clean it. Potatoes began in the earth
   Like Adam. A tuber, it knows its own worth.
Its texture and taste combine structure with matter.
It smells like the root that it is, and the weight
   Of its firm nubbly form feels right in the hand
   That holds it—familiar. An old trusted friend
A life-giving staple, a natural great.

Rice

My grandfather was a physician on a ship.
        While he was at sea, his daughters and his wife
        Sailed across on a trans-Pacific trip
Via Hawai'i to Japan. Their life

Thereafter included an Asian staple—rice.
        That alien favorite, after they all got home,
        Persisted as if inherited. It will suffice
To say all my children carry a chromosome

For rice. It's part of their nature. Assigned to make
        A rhyme about school, Willie wrote "Punahou
        Is nice/ Like a bowl of rice." The poem was fake,
The sentiment real, ingrained long ages ago.

So I'm not surprised that my grandchildren, half-Chinese,
Took to the food of their forebears with such ease.

Dishes

Are far too importunate. But paper cups
And plates are ecologically unsound
And cost too much. Sparkling glass and china—
To me not worth a daily waste of time
And water. Also dishwashers conceal
From sight the signal beauty of the task—
Soap bubbles catching rainbowed light.
                              It's true
That dishes need to be washed. My mother, though,
Taught me that housework should not interfere
With what matters more—a letter, a walk, a friend,
And other human pleasures we enjoy.

So I don't do dishes daily. Never have.
I wait until the inclination strikes.

My kitchen has a practical double sink
On one side deep enough for stacking plates
And pots and pans and glasses out of sight
Three days. After each meal I rinse things clean
And hide them there
                 until I want to play
In the bubbles, laze in the slippery sheen of foam
On china surfaces, revel in rainbows

Breaking all over. Meanwhile, half in a daze,
I slide my fingers around the familiar shapes
Of the silver, even admire how the water slips
From the faucet.
    It's not the chore itself I dislike—
Just the everlasting niggling of it.

A Daylight Discovery

Light slides to the cool enamel of the sink
Beneath the windowsill
And on the silver
Before I turn on the tap for hot water and suds.

How quiet the light is, spun to the surfaces
Of serviceable things.
                    Collected. Waiting.

Stilled, I admire the various ways of shining—
Luster in teacups, plainsong in standing goblets,
Sunlight pooling in spoons, glowing on porcelains,
The way the glasses catch clusters of light
On their smooth planes or diamond their faceted chips,
How motionless gleams seem to circle around in bowls.

A rush of water-sparkle and everything changes:

Dishes swimming in shimmers,
Reflections, spinning translations of color, bubbles
Shifting transparencies, sudden puddlings of light
When the water clears and closes over a ladle
Or slips into arcs upon the rims of glasses—
The very substance of light
Discovered
Washing the dishes.

Polishing Sugar Spoons

My filigreed sugar spoons look black,
Air-tarnished although they lie in a chest
With oddments of cutlery, wrapped in a stack
Of antique inherited silver. The crest

On one has scrolls with the name of my mother—
"Dorothy." Gothic, ornate, each letter
Comes clear when I rub them with polish. The other,
Far more complex in effect, I like better:

The crest: "Eureka!" The bowl: "Golden Gate"
With lighthouse and cutter. No bridge on the Bay.
The handle exhibits the name of the state,
And my grandmother's monogram—ECA—

Appears on the back with a pick and a spade.
It's history molded in silver days,
Souvenirs of San Francisco displayed
On old sugar spoons, an antique craze.

Tea and Coffee

That I'm equipped for coffee
Anyone could guess.
I have a small espresso
And a medium French Press,
A white ceramic filter,
And an automatic Krup,
An aluminum percolator,
And a sensible porcelain cup.
I buy coffee from the co-op
Fair traded for the store.
I grind the beans at breakfast—
A fragrance I adore.

Tea seems to me more formal,
More delicate in taste.
My teacups are more fragile,
Their decorations graced
With violets, lilies, mums,
Hand-painted on fine china,
And every teacup comes
Together with a saucer.
Flowers adorn the pot
A comfort and a ritual—
Fine tea served steaming hot.

Americans love coffee.
The English favour tea
That they're equally delicious
I'm likely to agree.
For right time and occasion
I choose whichever I will

And drink my fill.

Guests

I like to have guests in my house, to invite
        The people I care for. Impromptu or planned,
A lunch or a dinner, a bed for the night—
        I give what I have, nothing showy or grand,
For pleasure of friendship. My house is quite small,
        But I lay extra mattresses out on the floor,
Enough pillows and blankets and linens for all.
        It gets pretty cozy, with two, three or four.
I've even slept seven, with two in my bed
        And one in the cellar, and me on the couch,
And breakfast for all, which takes thinking ahead—
        Maple syrup and butter and pancakes from scratch.

Everyone helps as we clean up the mess,
        Our laughter the proof of domestic success.

Old Courtesies

Whenever I lay out places for ten
On the dining room table or lunch for just one,
My hands seek accustomed arrangements—the spoon
And the knife to the right, forks left. For wine
And for water two glasses, a napkin of linen

Close to the forks, a dish for the butter
Above, with its smooth knife, the other
Silver arranged beside it—oyster
Knife, nutpick, shrimpfork—all of those queer
And scarcely used gifts which I keep for the rare
Unlikely occasion, the crystal salt cellar
Within easy reach, the peppermill near.

*

I muse as I set the table. There come to my mind
Inherited formal patterns used as we dined:

Habitual manners a long time gone,
Like other behaviors either unknown
Or forgotten in present-day haste to be done—
"How do you do" with a nod, as a motion
Of greeting, no curtsy, no bowing down,
Seldom a handshake of warm recognition.

I also remember the old telephone
Which was answered by somebody friendly and known.
I loved getting letters handwritten by pen,
In ink on good paper, car doors held open
For passengers, old-fashioned courteous men
Who offered their seats to the frail and the laden,
Soft music, and smokers who ask or refrain,
Cordial young people who rise as a sign
Of respect—every departed convention.

All the old manners my parents taught me, my body,
Bemused, performs. Some kind of civility
Inherent in rituals lives on in my reverie.

Laundry

Nausicaa down by the stream long ago
      Lacked faucets for doing the wash, whereas we
Push a button for hot and cold water to flow.
      So easy! The washing machine leaves us free
Of grueling labor to do what we choose.
      We don't need a washboard. We don't need a tub.
The washing machine does the laundry. O Muse!
      Sing the pleasures of women who don't have to scrub.

Stains

Directions on how to remove any stain,
wherever it came from, abound. They assign
a solution for each, and I do not complain
of such recommendations. The methods are fine,

but they're never at hand in my need, and my brain
has registered only that pink and red wine
are countered by salt, and blood, by the plain
essentials of water and soap. I incline

toward the simple. Although I use bleach,
of dubious merit, I do realize
that lemon is helpful. And seldom in reach.
Three alternate methods may serve as disguise:
hide under a hankie or sew in a pleat
or toss in a rag pile. Acknowledge defeat.

Tangible Sunshine

No gas or electric dryers for me. They spin
        Dead air through clothes that don't smell clean, just hot.
 The scent of "Spring Flowers" or "Mint" that comes on a thin,
        Hankie-like fluffer (pink sugar perfume) is not
What I favor. I take delight in the fresh warm smell
        Of laundered things I gather off the line—
Blouses, underwear, napkins, sheets. I can tell
        How clean they are. The clothes in my arms make sunshine
Tangible. I can embrace it. Sweet air outside
        Can last for months, caught into the wash, line-dried.

Changing Times

I used to dislike ironing. It was a chore
    Both tedious and demanding, done by wives
Or servants in the past. That was before
    Nylon and polyester changed our lives
(Along with women's lib and civil rights).
    Fresh off the line, the wrinkled clothes heaped high,
Would wait for my attention—colors and whites—
    Till I'd be forced to iron, just to get by.

But time brought change in culture and in style.
    Ironing became for me an hour of leisure.
A warm smell rising from a steaming pile
    Of shirts and napkins, all the sensuous pleasure
Of cottons, woolens, silks. For I find such
    Sweet peacefulness in textures, comfort in touch.

Ironing: Sheets

After the weekly wash is clean and dry
And I've ironed the shirts, the slacks, the skirts, the blouses,

    I may tackle the oversize sheets, or at least I try
    To smooth out wrinkles. This futile effort arouses
        Frustration because they don't fit on the board.
        They droop to the floor and actively pick up dirt.
    They're too bulky to fold for the shelves. Besides, the cord
    Reaches only what rests on the flat of the board. So I squirt

The steam onto the cloth and iron what's handy—that's it.
Before I'm half finished, the job needs a mangle. I quit.

I'd rather
    sleep in wrinkles.
        In one
          n
           i
            g
             h
              t
                  The
          ironed
            s
             h
              e
               e
              t
               s

Get crumpled anyhow. Right?

Ironing: Curtains

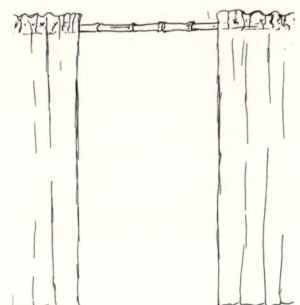

*Curtains too
Are hard to do.*

No more likely than sheets to fit the board
      They're equally likely to get mixed up in the cord.
Curtains and sheets have one main difference though:
      Sheets get hidden in blankets; curtains show.
That's the whole point. They keep out excess light
      And hide interiors, shield from strangers' sight
The private lives inside. Such functions mean
      That curtains should be decorative and clean
And smooth. That's a big order, calling for care,
      Effort, and space, worth leaving windows bare
For the whole process to happen.
                   Helpful to know
      That simply by hanging, draperies will grow
Smoother and straighter with time. A warning: more dust
      Will have to be dealt with next. It's well to adjust
A need to be smooth with an equal need to be clean
      For a curtain that serves a preference not to be seen.

Cleaning the Bathroom

Cleaning the bathroom is humbling and good.
Enamel and glass feel smoother than wood

as the mind, barely thinking, goes passive. Meanwhile
the hand, gliding easily over the tile

or toilet or mirror, finds tangible peace,
in the rhythm of rubbing, a kindly release

and the patience of porcelain fixtures can drain
what's flashy or fancy in favor of plain.

In style unpretentious, demeanor serene,
the bathroom is basic. Its function: to clean.

Clutter

The hardest domestic work that I do, the most
        Time consuming, is straightening the mess in a room
Before I clean it: all those loose papers tossed
        Onto tables, the books, the bags—whatever a broom

Or a vacuum might run into—wastebasket, shoe.
        The sweaters and scarves draped over the arm of a chair
Need to be folded and stashed, all the stuff that I threw
        In my haste to do something forgotten. The question is, where

Does everything rightfully fit? If I start out reading
        The letters I've saved, I tend to save them again.
And how can I throw away records I might be needing
        For next year's taxes? Too many decisions. The zen

Of detaching myself from a life of significant things
        Is too much for the hour or two I can spend. It brings
On a headache. The solution seems to be this: I hide
        All the stuff I've collected. In closets I lay it aside.

It can't go anywhere.
I leave all of it there.

Wooden Floors

Because I respect the floors of my house,
To kneel on the sounding boards feels good
As I sponge fresh water over the wood
Or rub in wax.
            They've borne for years
The weight of heavy furniture,
Scraping of chairs, the daily tread
Of light foot, bare or shod. Yet the floorboards
Still spring back. They're not like tile—
Solid—they have give, they yield.
And hold,
        and glow with a tea-colored sheen,
Rich under sunlight or lamplight, yet keep
A darkness integral to their tone.
The seams are narrow, the lines are clean
Where the boards were laid down level and joined
To form satiny planes. These floors

Are gouged in places, scored black crosswise
Here. And there, some kind of oil
Got spilled on the wood. And yet, the floors,
Outlasting all indignities, are beautiful.

Sensible of gratitude, to what I could not tell,
Mere hours before the birth of a child
I would kneel down and wash my wooden floors,
Working, tracing the grain with the palm of my hand,
Remembering trees they come from, what they are.
Afterwards I'd rise, sustained, at peace, into labor.

Sweeping

Rugs rise into a vacuum cleaner.
They get pulled up. They twist themselves
Around the engine, which spits out
A stink of burnt rubber, till I can't unplug
The connection fast enough. The smell
Hangs around polluting the air. Besides,
A vacuum won't let you see what you're doing.

Broom: so fit an implement:
A polished pole for a handle, gripped
Like a paddle's haft, the rhythm of sweeping—
Not fluid but lively. The stiff broom bristles
Discover the smutch, loosen and whisk it
Out to the floorboards—a cluster of refuse
To brush in a dustpan or sweep out the door.

A broom disturbs what's been tracked in
Unwanted, stirs up dirt, hurries it
Into plain sight and deals with it smartly.
Though the dust settles back, a good broom
Lets you see what was there before you got at it.
Serviceable, light, and plain, it keeps me
Honest . . .

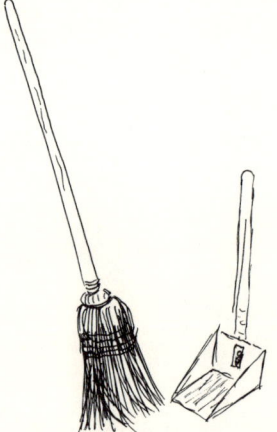

Domestic Violence

I care for the Oriental rugs I own
By beating then hosing them down to dry in the sun.
Such acts of domestic violence have been shown
To have brightened the rich, warm colors when I am done.

Dust

A soft film
dulls the shine of old furniture.
The light in the wood—oak, mahogany, cherry—
has been saved inside rockers, tables, bookcases.
It marks the weavings of sun into leaf cells,
breathes with a history of trees.

By itself, dust hurts nothing it covers,
its touch on wood milder than sunshine
or cold. I do not mind it.
                            Sometimes,
rubbing with oil the familiar pieces,
shaking the soft cloth free,
I mull over thoughts of the one death
encountered by every living thing,
unavoidable and still ahead,
body become dust, trees felled or fallen.

My hand slows, polishing wood as I muse,
but I feel no fear—only an evanescent sadness—
understanding, as I must,
all creation as dust.

Indoor Plants

My mother did not approve of indoor plants.
She thought them tasteless, and I don't know why.
I have just one—a spider plant hung high
Near the kitchen window above the sink. It slants

Southward toward daylight. Once I had mint in a pot
On a plant stand, growing in soil. Assailed by a strong
Unpleasant smell, I observed before very long
That the cats had chosen mint over litter box. Not

That I really blame them. But now I have good reasons
To grow all my flowers outside in appropriate seasons.

An Improbable Forest

A scent of lemon oil, its slight tang
In the air when I lift the bottle out to the counter,
Mingles with odors of soap, and before I begin,
A concept of "clean" is released in the kitchen.
I can nearly smell it.

And I can feel it
In the soft cloth of this old tee shirt,
As if I were holding a cloud,
Or a bundle of poppy petals.
One squirt of polish
Dampens the whole handful.
But not as water would, not wet, and smoother.

Then I begin to rub the beautiful woods
Of my furniture—walnut Victorian sofa and chairs,
Mahogany dining room table, cherrywood bedstead,
Dresser and rocking chair of light-colored oak,
And the heavy pine mantel over the brick fireplace.

Dreamily, as I linger over the finials
Of the antique plant stand, rubbing in furniture oil,
I imagine all these trees green, alive
Together—along with sandalwood, birch, and koa,
Eucalyptus, elm—in a matchless improbable forest.
All those trees.
                I go deep into that forest.
That teaches me ways to handle the things I love.

Holding On

I want to keep all of it—towels of old linen
Embroidered in white, PH, DAH, ECA,
And hemmed with prinked margins, ironed,
Hanging in the bathroom over white bars,
The walnut chairs in the study, no one like another,
Scrolled with particular roses, acorns, dogwood,
Monogrammed silver shining on a shining table,
Plantstands with finials, bedstead carved with grapes,
Threadbare Persian rugs, tapa from Fiji.

I know you can't take it with you. I know what Death
Told Everyman: *Salvation relies on good deeds*. But things
Are good deeds. They glow into the coming years
Quietly. I want them near to me. Forever.
No gimcrack—my great-grandmother's emerald ring,
My amber pendant, the dark Victorian furniture,
Even worn sheets, and the watch my father wore.

Things keep secrets. Somehow I know what they are.

Fireplace

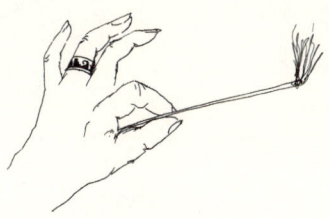

Since a genuine fireplace needs to burn genuine wood,
I've collected dry branches and sticks whenever I could.

Old beams and lengths of lath and left-over boards
From do-it-yourself construction, handcut cords

Piled up in the yard. Inside, a crumpled batch
Of paper. Rasp of a wooden "strike anywhere" match.

Sparkles like tiny stars. One flame. Then fire!
And the heaped stack catches, sharp and soft as desire.

How is it that fire can be silken and stinging keen,
Both colored and clear? Savage and civilized? Green,

Scarlet, orange, saffron, ice-water blue,
And the transparent, colorless, vivid shivering hue

Of pure light rising, drawn to air, to black.
Those fires at the sills of primeval caves far back

In our rank beginnings, left nothing. Or ashes. Space
And time were bare theory, gone in fire. As the place

For the quickening flame burns what I've saved, I stare
At the fire, musing on nothing. Nothing is there.

Their Quietness

The quietness
of things that do not move of themselves—
table, paper, doorknob, waterglass—
draws my thought. It is as if
they were waiting.

Inclined. Patient.
They are.
They do not offer their being.
They do not ask anything.
They are familiar to my touch.
When I lift my grandmother's silver hairbrush,
or pull the lamp chain or push the curtains back,
or hold my pen in my fingers,
I do not regard them.

I would like to carry with me
familiar things
to whatever heaven there may be,
not out of pride or greed or ownership,
only because of their quiet attendance—
because of how they live.

I Suspect My Subconscious Is On To Something

I lose things too often—essentials, not frills—
My glasses, my checkbook, my keys,
My wallet, my charge cards, old numbers, new bills—
There's little so needed as these.

Misplacing a shirt or a cup or a book
For a matter of hours or days—
No problem, there's always one more. But to look
For what I need now—that plays

Pure havoc with every good feeling and thought
Since all that exists in my mind
Is a replicate image of what I have sought
Without being able to find.

Though so far I've always located what's lost
All the frustrated time that I waste
Subtracts from the value and adds to the cost
Of the various things I've misplaced.

I'm told that my psyche is sending a clue:
What I lose I don't want. I admit that it's true.
Letting go obligations is what I'd prefer.
To be carefree and cheerful. I wish that I were.

Dealing With the Trash

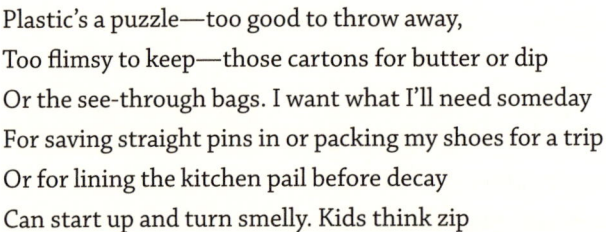

I feel quite satisfied about the trash:
A weekly schedule, an enormous bin,
And I am shut of garbage, waste, and ash,
Especially paper—all the post brings in
Of ads and notices, appeals for cash—
Plus cat food cans, old bones, banana skin.

Plastic's a puzzle—too good to throw away,
Too flimsy to keep—those cartons for butter or dip
Or the see-through bags. I want what I'll need someday
For saving straight pins in or packing my shoes for a trip
Or for lining the kitchen pail before decay
Can start up and turn smelly. Kids think zip

Is worth saving, and I wish I could throw out more,
Since chucking refuse makes me feel flighty, free
As a teen. But trained to recycling during The War,
I remain frugal, in sync with the latest *esprit*
De temps. Still, as an old woman I cannot ignore
The final divestment—my body as rubbish to be—

Empty as any wastebasket the day before
My final trash pickup for all of eternity.

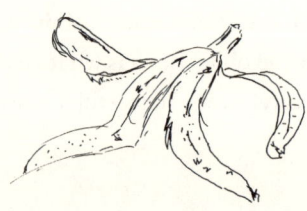

Recycling

Plastic containers, newspapers, glass,
Aluminum soda cans, cardboard, and all
That used to be useless now wait in a mass
For the bins at the recycling place in the mall.

As I separate items, put each in its pile,
I consider how governments, dealing with trash,
Convert it to service again, and I smile
In the positive job of negating my stash.

Stitchery

Thirty years ago in winter in Chartres
When we were young and ignorant, able,
With time to travel, realize a map,
We climbed a stairway to a garret, rented
For the night.
              One bureau. Two white beds
With sheets of heavy linen, sweetly mended
In minuscule stitches, barely detectable patches
Smooth as the fabric.
                And I dreamed of a peerless maiden
Sewing by lamplight.
                And I dreamed of a widow mending
By day her wedding sheets, her patient care
To keep old linens beautiful for white beds
Where strangers sleep.
              I lack that delicate skill.
I cannot piece out patterns, or embroider,
Or mend sheets.
          I rub under my thumb
Monograms my mother stitched on towels
Years ago, and never dreamed of strangers.

Knitting

How smooth the feel
        of wooden knitting needles
Moving in my fingers
        flicking the woolen yarn
Down and over
        in the primal rhythms of a motion
As easy as singing.
        Quiet, I grow comfortable
So to be joined
        by threads to my forebears, women
Knitting in the sun
        at windows of cottages and shacks,
Nearly idle.
        Thoughts briefly rising and falling
Graze the pattern
        emerging as I stitch
        and may change it,
Though I keep to the overall shapes
        that hands have known
Of themselves for centuries so well
        I seldom look down.
My mind, become peaceable, can listen
        to the silence of the ages
Till I find in the blunted click
        of the wooden needles
The music of the poetry I live by.

Bookworms

I thought a bookworm only a metaphor
For pedantry, till I found five worms in a book
Chewing a path through Dickens. When one good look
Uncovered the tiny wrigglers attempting to bore
Little holes in the paper, I squashed them. Real readers enjoy
Collections of words that bookworms can destroy.

I'd squash them again if I found them
Eating my books—I'd pound them.

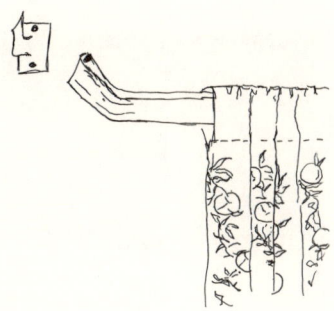

Brackets and Rods

Sometimes I need to put up a rod with a bracket.
The job appears simple—just grab a nail and whack it:

But first find the tape or the yardstick and carefully measure
The span between two spots. Because of the pressure

To get it right, I get it wrong each time—
Too long or too short for the curtain rods. I climb

The step ladder anyhow, carrying fixtures—nails
In my pocket, the hammer at hand. But it never fails:

When I pound in a nail to the bracket I hold on the spot,
The nail goes in crooked. But since it's not off by a lot

I hammer the other. With luck I may force it to stay
Though the angle's all wrong, and the prongs get themselves in my way.

When it sticks for a minute, at least temporarily,
I harbor a hope that if I act warily,

Hanging and parting the curtains or raising the shade,
My set-up perhaps will conceal the botch that I've made.

My bracket may last for a year or a day.
I fold up the ladder and put it away.

Putting Up Art

As I hang up a painting, once again I know
    Why I need art. There are things words cannot say,
Thoughts that the eyes can see. My paintings show
    Ideas invisible any other way.

I knock a small nail into the plaster, change
    Daniel's snowlit lavender trees for a pale
Soft pink triangular angel, rearrange
    An abstract Allen lithograph on the rail

Over the fireplace, beside Ichinose's bowl
    Of featherlight koa. Dark Fijian tapa
Covers the door between the calligraphy scroll
    And Rosen's coral and apricot *Madonna*.

Today, McCauley's French window: the rose-fallen light
    Echoes a lost aubade, a way of being.
I lift the picture, position the wire just right,
    And drift off into the life I live by seeing.

The In-House Pet

A whole new ball game is the domestic pet.
We love it in spite of how it may behave.
They all start out with trips to see the vet,
And then they settle in at home. We save

The left-over bones and scraps from our own meal
For them. We're glad to be of use. But dogs
Need daily walks. They train us till we feel
Our duty is our privilege, our pay—wags,

Not wages. We ignore bad breath, and drool.
It's love we learn from dogs. And cats—we find
As they quickly adapt to a litter box, how cool,
How neat, they are, how proud. But they leave behind

All over the house the pieces of litter their paws
Pick up. Housekeeping becomes a delicate chore
Of littered bits. Cat fur and dog hair also cause
Vexation, attracted to carpets, sofas, the floor,

And all dark clothing. Such troubles have often tried
Our affection, no matter how hard we've denied
That they distress us. Each of us needs to decide
Whether a pet is our problem or our pride.

The Cat and the Computer

I have a computer and I have a cat.
        They tangle together; they're safer apart.
Ace rubs up against me. I give him a pat
        And head to my study. I'm ready to start

When Ace jumps on to the mouse pad. He licks
        And examines his forepaws. He's planning to stay.
But cats and computers are not a good mix.
        I lift him back down. I nudge him away.

He springs to my lap. He leaps on to the keys—
        A major mistake. Destructive as dust,
The hair of the cat from antics like these
        Can gum up the works with a vengeance. I thrust

My dadblasted cat off the table. I'm vexed
        As my hands hit the keyboard, while Ace stretches out
As limp as a rug on the floor. So what's next?
        A pounce on the printer? My light-legged lout—

A troublesome typist, a skilled acrobat—
His verve I deplore. But I do love my cat.

Divided Joy

I see how the slanting sunlight upon the windows
Illuminates rain-lines of dust streaking the panes
And I have a mind to transparency. I mix vinegar
And water in a pail and go to the cellar for newspapers.
This is the happiest job we do together, you and I:

I'm outside where ragged sparkles slop out of the pail.
You're in the house, moving around the furniture.
We meet on the chilly glass. We wet it, it drips
To the sill. And now the rattle of crunching newspaper.
It sings taking up water, and squeals. Our hands
Keep finding smudges. We smile at each other, shrug
And rub the panes some more, and buff the surface
Clear. You signal, and I move over one
And we polish the next close by, and the one after that.

I love how we bring the colorless glass to a shine
Apart from each other, how we find the not-quite reflections
Of one another on either side, like a mirror,
But not, our hands together, untouching, describing
The same circles, our laughter fizzing upwards
To the same clarity, the same divided joy.

Getting the Mail

As if the mail might deliver a marvel, I wait
For letters daily, a little at loose ends
Until they arrive. What I anticipate
I do not know. Some company usually sends

Catalogues, ads, or bills. Even these
Release my tension. Rifling through the mail
I trash the ads, tend to the frequent pleas
For charity, pay my bills, but never fail

To look for a magic message that may surprise
My spirit, break open my life, change everything.
It does not come. Daily the post denies
My fiction that years will yield sweet secrets, bring

Amazing news—the grace of a happy end
To a human story, a pledge and a promise granted,
A trust recovered, a love requited, a friend—
In the letter that offers me all I have ever wanted.

Noises

      i Inside noise

Water splashing into the kitchen sink.
The furnace thrumming along. The telephone.
The swamp-cooler pump. Refrigerator. Drone
Of a coasting fly. The muted, soapy clink

Of silver on porcelain. A rotating fan.
Pop of a toaster. Unwelcome TV blare.
The clocks. The pencil sharpener. Scrape of a chair.
A boiling egg bumping around in the pan.

A page being turned. The click of a closing drawer.
The burr of a quiet computer. A window shade
Being raised. A toilet flushing. A radio played.
A doorbell ringing. Swush of an opening door.

      ii And all of the noise outside:

One way or another, the numberless sounds outside
Have mostly to do with human locomotion.
Vehicular travel reflects a heady devotion
To driving a car or a truck or taking a ride

On a bike or a skateboard, wagon or bus. And each
Is marked by a certain recognizable feel
In its rattle or whine, its hiss or skitter or squeal—
A mode of expression, a typical kind of speech.

The police car siren's summons, the rises and falls
And clangs of the fire engine's warning alarms, the train's
Diminishing whistle, the overhead roar of planes,
Church bells, lawn mowers, ice cream trucks, bird calls—

Oh birds! their songs, their warbles, their tremulos—
Unique—their feathers, the low-flying wheeling wings.
The muddy, mumbling river. The wind that sings
Or blusters or whispers, or soughs or sighs as it blows.

Bees in hives or burrowing inside flowers
Do not sound like flies. The burner in a balloon
Does not sound like a stove. Dogs bay at the moon
But can whimper or bark or growl all twenty-four hours.

Changes of weather: Fog-hush. Rhythms of rain—
Sheets, drops. Thunder—rumble, roll or gun.
The sound-enshrouding snow. The baking sun
Quietly breaking the earth apart again.

      iii Inside and Outside: Human Noises

Sounds of the body—scuff and slide of feet
In leather soles, of bounce in rubber. Cries
Of happiness. Chuckles. Moans. Laments. Deep sighs
Of pain or sadness. Bland and bitter and sweet—

Even in thought, the body responds with breath,
Motion, speech, music. We have a noise
For every activity, all of our sorrows and joys.
The sounds we make cease only in our death.

Bird Feeding

The sparrows flutter on currents of air
And fold their wings at the seed.
The hummers spin down, then hover near
The liquefied sugar they need.

The sugar dissolved in the water I pour,
The beads of birdseed I spoon,
Collect feisty hummers—they always want more—
And keep sparrows chirping in tune.

In winter I put out more birdseed, but nothing for hummers.
They're only around in the summers.

Cutting the Blue Grama Grass

Even with xeriscape, the lawn needs mowing,
The desert sun beats down, the grass keeps growing.

Dry as the earth is, the thin stalks survive.
Brown in the winter, summer lets them thrive.

While I push the mower, grass-green scents arise.
And the work, when it's done, delights and gratifies.

A fragrance out of Eden colors the air.
While the grass keeps right on growing everywhere.

Painting the House

The day that my realtor pulled up to the curb
I discovered the place where I knew I could spend
The rest of my life. "Now *there* is a house
I could live in," I said. Already a friend,

An old fixer-upper exactly my age,
Advertised as "a jewel," it needed fresh paint
Both inside and out. I bought it, and then
Bought ladder and brushes, observed no restraint

In the buckets of color I chose for my life—
Sun-yellow the base, deep green for the trim.
When I put up the ladder and tackled my task
My neighbors would notice me out on a limb

Or a ladder. They'd loiter, surprised but distressed
By a woman up under the eaves with her hand
On a brush which she dipped into paint and slapped onto
The woodwork. "Don't worry. It's just as I planned,"

I told them. And when it was done
I threw a big party in yellow and green,
Avocados and cheeses, limeade and champagne,
Green mints, yellow cakes. Every shade in between

Was worn by my guests. And over the hill
A full moon rising, its tranquil light
Infusing peace. It lingers still—
The sweet celebration of that night.

Fixers

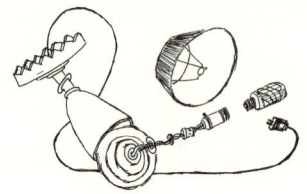

In any house things can go wrong—
        Electricity goes bad, a window cracks.
The grama grass gets too long.
        A sliding closet door slips off its tracks.

Plumbing stops up or leaks.
        The telephone won't work. The furnace fails.
If household trouble peaks
        With tasks too heavy or hard for old females,

It's time for a fixer—Ken
        Or Rafael. They're skilled and quick. I call
For help and get it when
        I need it. Some jobs I cannot handle, small

Or large. I'm glad to pay
        For a screened in porch, fresh paint, a ceiling light,
A lock—any thing any day.
        They do what I want, and they always do it right.

Besides, they leave things neat
        When the work is done. I know I'll need them again,
But I've lived on Easy Street
        Ever since I lucked onto two good handymen.

Ants

Ants are amazing, of course; they also annoy.
They go for our scraps. They work out a tidy assault
On unsealed caches of food which they enjoy.
They seize on spills in the kitchen—clearly my fault

If I fail to change an old gasket or cover a crack
On closed containers. Ants use signals. They spread
The word, then form two lines—to come and go back
To wherever they live. They carry their crumbs of bread

Home to their hill. My book calls them "organized"
And "social," "industrious." They're more like "pest"
And "infestation." I want to be advised
About how to get rid of them all, to leave *my* nest,

Return to theirs. I don't, though I'd like to, spray.
I'm afraid that they're somehow useful to neighbor and friend,
That I'm not being "green." So I hurry them on their way
By hiding my food, leaving them no dividend,
No message to send. To come to their end
                         is what I intend.

Moths

The beauties of clothes made of "organic" cloth
are victims to soft depredations of moth.

Cotton and feathers and fur don't survive
The specialized larvae which eat them alive.

And wool. And silk. We have to take care
To keep caterpillars off things that we wear

Or get eaten through by a greedy varmint.
Moth holes can appear in our favorite garment.

Dry cleaning and moth balls and strong plastic bags
Can keep our good clothing from turning to rags.

Though it's not always easy to pack things away,
We can shield what we have from too early decay.

Beginner's Kit: Bees

They arrived in a package by regular U.S. mail
with seven or ten clinging on to the screen outside
that kept the rest of them in.
The postman who handed them over said,
"Don't worry, they won't leave the queen.
See? Inside the little container."

I worried—receptive but unfamiliar with bees.

The first surprise—
how loud those bugs were buzzing inside the screens,
and next, their fury—tiger-colored bodies
crowding around transparent sugar water
after I dumped the whole "beginner's kit"
into the hive, all three pounds of bees,
then cautiously poked out the wax,
opened the tiny cage where the queen resided,
and hung it securely above and put back the roof.

Nothing to do, said the book, but wait and watch
and keep the feeder full of sugar-water
for the several weeks the workers need
for building combs for the brood
while the queen fills the cells.

*   *   *

A wonder! Down thousands of years
they've know what to do with their lives
and how to do it,
how to tunnel in pollen of apple bloom,
how to suck sweet drops of nectar from cactus and clover,
to seal off tiny exact hexagonal cells
all filled with honey or brood.

Everybody for everybody under one queen,
brood and food and protection.
What a seductive existence!

But I prefer my freedom to watch
and walk away into a life I choose,
which includes my bees.

Packing for Travel

Whenever I go away on a trip
        I pack an old suitcase the day before—
Blouses and slacks, a dress and a slip,
        Underwear, two pairs of shoes or more,
Toothbrush and toothpaste, pills and a sweater,
        Ear plugs for the airplane, comb and hairbrush—
Whatever I think I might want. It's much better
        A day in advance—there's no need to rush.

I try to prepare for what might take place,
        Formal or casual, sneakers or heels,
By chance or arrangement, exalted or base,
        Dining with candles or bolting down meals.
But no matter how careful the plans in my mind,
        I notice I never use all that I picked,
That somehow I always leave something behind
        And come home with more than I packed. I predict

That I won't give up hoping to pack my bag right
With all that I need and still travel light.

Shopping

When I come home from traveling somewhere foreign,
Shame drives me quickly past supermarket shelves
Bulging with packages screaming in red and yellow
To be bought. Sometimes I cannot look,
Even, at excessive dietary supplements
And five brands of toothpaste, soap, lipstick, and soup cans,
Or adorable babies bubbling on bottles of syrup,
Glossy dogs smiling from dog-food bags, shoe polish,
Matches, motor oil, brooms, candy, hair spray.

I cannot stand the great American pastime.
It bores me. Still, I have to buy what I need.

                But I don't need much.

Though I buy what my car requires at any gas station,
I get new clothes from irrepressible catalogues,
Or from second-hand shops where there's seldom more than one
Of whatever it is. It's like finding a four leaf clover,
Instead of being "helped" by well-groomed ladies
In empty department stores. I'm baffled by rows
Of identical dresses in different sizes and colors,
All costing the earth.
                For food I prefer my markets

Outside—apples that grew on actual apple trees,
Have bruises, taste like apples, not schoolroom paste,
Potatoes that came dirty from the earth. Grapes
Warmed where they drooped in clusters, darkly shaded
From sun under coarse vine leaves. Peas in pods,
Not wrapped in plastic bags and labeled "English."
I raise tomatoes in my own back yard.

The worst affront to my natural predisposition
Was being advised that to shop after nine eleven
Was an act of patriotism—to me an arrogance
Insulting as whining "Why do they hate us so."

Still, I do have to buy things, but I choose my sources:
My favorites are flea markets, thrift shops, auctions,
Co-ops, roadside stands and yard sales. What
I prefer is a find dependent on good fortune
And good sense.

Taxes

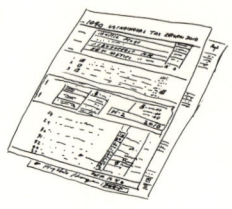

My property taxes are billed to me twice every year—
A month before Christmas, a month before summer vacation.
I pay them on time. I prefer that my house remain clear
Of financial arrears, so I handle my real obligation

To all public servants—the cops and the firemen who
Are required to remain on call both days and nights
To keep citizens safe. I underwrite projects too
Which taxes support—the schools, the streets, all the rights

That government guarantees. Our taxes get spent
On public communal jobs that need to be done.
Though it's not always easy to see where the money went,
It benefits all though we pay for it one by one.

Accepting that obligation makes me feel strong.
I'm happy to play my part. (Besides, I must.)
But misappropriation is rampant and wrong,
And crime like rain falls both on just and unjust.

A sign I admired that I saw at a crowd's demonstration
Stated my sentiment: "Taxes are patriotic."
The money assessed on a people finances a nation
When it's spent on what's needed and not on what's vain or exotic.

I hate being had. Examples: I don't like the onus
Of paying with taxpayers' funds some rich banker's bonus
Or of building a bridge to nowhere.
I don't want to go there.

But I'm happy to pay
To keep trouble away.

My Back Door

My back door opens on an untended yard.
        No grass or plants. The ground is bare and hard.
A wooden fence conceals me from the sight
        Of friendly next door neighbors, left and right,
As well as from back alley drifters I can hear
        Chatting or wrangling while they drink their beer.

The yard's not empty, though. I've planted a pear,
        A cherry, two apples, a fig, and over there
By my bedroom window a resolute cottonwood.
        Each one of these has grown as high as it should.

Close to the backyard gate beside the fence
        I've put up a clothesline, since it makes more sense
To dry all my laundry outside in the sun
        Than in an electric dryer, and when it's done
It smells like flowers.
                But what draws the eyes
        Is the arbor, its bunches of grapes a hidden surprise,
Purple beneath their tender leaves. Two hives
        Nearby still shelter my bees who spend their lives
In golden honey. Wild birds coast by for seed
        In the feeders, while cats gratify an inborn need
For neighboring felines to visit, to sit and gaze
        At each other.
                Spring, summer, and fall.

                    The days
Of winter, though, turn somber, brief, and cold.
        I go inside, letting my thoughts enfold
My life in hope. For a season the yard will keep.
        I close the door. I gather my house for sleep.

Acknowledgements

Divided Joy, *In Company,* University of New Mexico Press, 2007
Artichoke, *Artichoke and Other Poems,* University of Hawaii Press, 1969

Because I love my house as I might love a genial friend, I can love and celebrate my housework. The poems brought together in this collection, except for "Divided Joy," all center on the thoughts of a person working alone, even when someone else may live in the same house in close association with a housekeeper, even when a particular job such as dishwashing or putting up curtain rods may frequently involve one or two helpers.

The poems observe or disparage or celebrate the many occasions when a domestic encounter may give rise to feelings of quiet thoughtfulness or annoyance or pleasure, feelings which may be both strong and private.

That is why the poems express the responses of one person separated, by being engaged in a job, from any possible helpful companions. Yet such responses may well be universally shared by other experienced and happy housekeepers. I hope that will happen.